POETRY NOW

HOMELESS

Edited by Veronica Hannon

First published in Great Britain in 1993 by
POETRY NOW
1-2 Wainman Road, Woodston,
Peterborough, PE2 7BU

Foreword

Homelessness is an issue that has many political connotations and has become an issue of serious debate. Sometimes, though, we forget the individual suffering as we deal with the situation en masse.

The poets in this anthology refuse to let us forget the personal plight that is suffered by thousands nationwide. They speak with sympathy, understanding and without hesitation about some of the dreadful occurrences that happen on our very own streets.

So open these pages and let your heart and mind be touched by the tales these poets tell.

Contents

Passage Man

My distance drew nearer. And his eyes drowsy
focused on me like a torch in the dark.
His tilted head shelved on his shoulder. Crouching
the passage corner, he held his written voice.

Homeless, please spare some change.

I met his sorrow.

Left to support his belly through loss of self respect.
His upside down hat empty. Cast aside like an
unwanted cur to pace the streets. Invisible to his
fellow men. Thought of as scum, a fool, yet with
more to preach than you and I.

How hard his heart must be. Carved by the hands
of this wine society. Devoid of being. Laughed at by
passing little seeds who will grow insensitive to
misery.

Gently, I placed some silver colours in his bowl
shaped hands, and received his comely nod.
His mutter obliged.

And I reached the passage end. There, a well fed
busker (musician), his upside down hat full with
Change . . .
. . . ?

Mark Cachia

1

Bullring

A bullring serves as a field.
A bizarre series of plots.
Negotiated.

Walking towards a South Bank.
Across.

A river splitting Capital.
Asunder.

Here at the base of things.
Where sky and exhaust converge.

A bullring is a battle field.
Of farcical proportions.
Negotiated.

Where concrete equals mud.
Determined.

There are other armies encamped.
Invisible.

Tim Brennan

Empty Homes

Discarded mussel shells - bilateral
like fat fossilised butterflies
or petrified pea-pods
with smooth, shiny
mother of pearl
magical blue lining
- lately vacated.

On the outside,
barnacle colonies cluster
like extinct volcanoes,
or inverted moon craters
rising up in white desolate clumps
from the calciferous ground
- empty homes on the back
of an empty home.

June Handford

3

Runaway

And in the City today
Children of Eros sweetly play
And for the likes of those who pay
Stimulation.

A smoky squat, a single bed
A dirty coverlet is spread
To hide the loss of maidenhead
Degradation.

A pretty face can do a deal
There's clothes to buy and shoes to heel
If times get tough then for a meal
Submission.

And if a day of turning tricks
Has the emotions in a mix
There's always someone who can fix
The isolation.

And in the back streets a cardboard castle is burning
Shivers on the sidewalk, near a baker's, two young faces - masked -
Eyes yearning.

For it takes more than bread to satisfy the emptiness of the runaway
And it takes more than love and trust when these things have
                                                        been lost

At home.

Take me home.

Anne Storey

Goulston Street Baths

As boys slither near the 'Out of Order' lavatory
Urine seeps
From the Changing Room showers

We puddle through
Black grit
Mixed with liquid lamb's liver
To freshen our feet for the Pool

T Simon Couzens

5

Neglected Consequence of Urbanisation

On streets homeless sleep,
In boxes, in blankets on cold concrete.
From pavements outside to underground stations,
Spreads this neglected consequence of urbanisation.
Any amount of politics cannot make it subside.
Will Government drown society in a problem it denies?
Those in poverty beg for pennies to support their life,
What Government gives financially must be punishable crime.
Generous citizens; a monetary lifeline to those in need,
Government would rather see the poor deceased.
Charities who bring the homeless blankets and food,
Do not receive from Government any gratitude.
For themselves what can the homeless reap?
Except a vicious circle of poverty.
A failure of capitalism is what they exhibit,
Materials values to them are pathetic.
Everything concerned with commercialism and profit,
Is human life so worthless it is easily forgotten?
Still Government drowns society in a problem it denies,
All the amount of politics cannot make it subside.
But a rectification of the economic situation
May help lower the homeless population.
Look out your flat, house, mansion, five star hotel,
Explain what you see, describe the living hell;
A flowing neglected consequence of urbanisation,
Swamps pavements outside to underground stations.
In boxes, in blankets on cold concrete,
On streets, must homeless still sleep?

Soman Balan

Camden on Market Day

We stumbled on them by accident,
Turning away from a market for artisans
And walking in and out of a Parisian Bistro
We found them
           Sat on steps.

Behind the fruit stall, broken-shoed,
Stubbled, wearing junk clothes beneath
Long macs that flashers wear.
They sat there
           Eating from paper plates.

Or soiled handkerchiefs, that small space
Between hand and mouth that is the hungry.
With eyes that mock yet provoke pity
They saw us
           Stopped for a moment;

Stole from us our fluent footsteps, aware
Of the penetration of their eyes, then returning
To the hollow that is their life. Turning
We left them.

David Hawkins

Homeless

Sell me something if you want,
But I warn you, it had better be worth it.

The pile of ashes that I once called my life
Lies still and cold now;
And I, the ghost of something passed
Hold out my empty hand and ask
You to be kind enough to spare a coin
That I might eat tonight.

The pavements feel so hard today
And there's nowhere to sit but down.
So I sit on the ground, companion to the street rats
And undesirables that have made this their territory.
'Take me in and help me,' I beg,
But the only answer is a mocking laugh
And the stare of a bright orange eye,
Or silence.
Silence that strikes deep into my veins,
That releases the endless flow of salt tears;
Silence that produces my misery untold.

I live in a land of plenty,
A land that does not care for me.
I am a shadow which is hidden in dark corners
Because you don't want to know I exist.

Try to sell me something, if you like,
But I warn you, you won't have much luck.
I cannot buy what I need.

Navahra Lindsay

Sanctuary

No, I'll not envy him, whoever he be,
That stands upon the battlements of state;
Stand there who will for me,
I'd rather be myself than great.
Of being high the pleasure is but small
But long the ruin, if I chance to fall.

Let me in some spring park serenely lie,
Happy in leisure and obscurity;
While others place their joys
In popularity and noise.
Let my soft minutes glide obscurely on,
Like hidden urban streams, unheard, unknown.

Then when my days are all in silence past
A good plain Londoner I'll die at last.
Death cannot choose but be
To him a mighty misery
Who to the world was popularly known
And dies a stranger to himself, alone.

C M Wood

Nature's Friend Society's Outcast

Where does she go?
Where does she live?
How does she make her shoes and clothes?
How did she evolve into the state she's now in;
An outcast to society,
A no-hoper,
A sad case.

She stumbles along, her possessions in hand.
Her mumbled conversation, of many she's had.
Perhaps she talks of how she became . . .
But our ears are closed,
For we've already passed the blame.

She wasn't always like this, the way she is now.
Once upon a time, she was just like you and I,
Lived in accommodation, had enough to eat
Learnt how to read and write,
And conversated with human beings.

Now all she has to talk to,
Is herself and to the trees,
Nature does not pass judgement,
But sees things as they ought to be.

Simple, but a saviour,
Old as time itself,
Provides a forever lasting of friendship
And shelter under a branch.
Nature has kept her alive.
For human beings, her own kind . . .
Have already killed her.

Faustina Regina Cofie

The Economy of the State

(Some of us think we are really badly off - and some of us are really badly off.)

Central heating, running water
Light at the touch of a button
Please leave a message on the ansaphone
I'm out all day - shopping.
Is there something I've forgotten?

We think we've got everything
And then we want some more.
Give that poor man on the street
A pound. That will settle the score.

What - no foreign holiday this year?
Isn't it a shame
You ask me why hasn't she got a home?
Well - I'm certainly not to blame!

Juliet Formby

Terminal Inertia

In a padlocked office doorway,
she saw a heap of dirty washing,
starting as it moved.
Then half a grizzled head
and one dead eye appeared,
above the fraying, faded blanket,
staring through her at the rain
as though she were not there at all.

Thoughts of crossing over
cancelled out by guilt, she walked,
keeping, on the rim of vision,
his emaciated frame
as a man emerged
or what had once been called a man:
yawning, scratching, rubbing eyes
but slowly
as these exertions seemed beyond him
or every action vain.

'Got any change?' he mouthed
the words at her in passing.
Her face snapped blank;
fear no longer written there.
stripped of his identity
he'd lost all authority,
survival swallowed up his energy,
she saw he posed no threat, and yet

still flinched, assaulted by the waste
of his untasted youth.

Lyn S Westerman

Cardboard Box Hotel

I'm sleeping on the Southbank cause I've no place else to go,
Cardboard boxes everywhere homeless row by row;
Sold my watch for pizza now I've nothing left to sell.
So I'm sleeping on the Southbank in the cardboard box hotel.

London rich man's city where the rich get richer still,
Poor get even poorer paying rich man's phoney bills;
They rip me off for everything, life's a living hell,
Sleeping rough in cartons in a cardboard box hotel.

When I rise up in the morning, the mist hangs like a veil,
My bones are creaking hinges and I slop out in my pail,
I used to get a breakfast being a vagrant in the jail,
Now I'm free, I've got the freedom, of a cardboard box hotel.

Big new fancy jaguars when yuppies come to call,
They urinate their champagne on cardboard next the wall,
And tho' policemen saw them, they say they cannot tell,
If they urinated on me in my cardboard box hotel.

The social does not know me and the pains of living show,
My head's sore, and my feet're on fire, tramping to and fro'.
When Jesus wrote my horoscope he bid me fare-thee-well,
And dumped me with the cats and rats, in cardboard box hotel.

There are some who cannot take it, their hearts break and they cry,
Like the old who never make it, they just go to sleep and die;
Great Land of Hope and Glory, I've learned your lesson well;
Any hope that's for the homeless, is a cardboard box hotel.

Eddie Graham

In Need of Treatment

White/Male/Suburban/Clueless

Labels come flying into my face
Telling me I don't belong to this place.
Telling me I don't share the experience
That I know fuck all about being homeless.
I agree - and there's my point.

The Big Issue isn't for me the thousands that are homeless
But the millions that seem happy to leave them there.
Often saying ' . . . they made themselves homeless!'
'Sure some are in need . . . *But!*
Suggesting the rest are there for the fun of it!
What a sick society we've become. Clueless
Even to the glue that holds us together.
I am beginning to see myself as part of the disease!

Perhaps it's naive to say we should care
Perhaps it's time we needed a scare.
After all it's only another market -
The trade in human misery has an ancient pedigree
It's what we understand - Fear and Greed.
It's all about being afraid to bleed.

It'll take a lot for us commuters
To take off the blinkers - our fiercesome focus
We need to get to work.
But that's only an excuse
Even if you turn your head away
The smell of piss will have it's say
It's not as if we don't notice.
We choose not to - and that's my point.

White/Male/Suburban/Clueless
Can't somebody help me!

G A Stewart

14

The Straggler

Me home is a drum
A dirty blackened, battered
Flaming diesel drum
And a plank
And a tin or two
Where I can rest me bum
To swig from the neck of a naggin
Belonging to a chum
And see the stars a shining
And the moon and the sun
With a sip for a fellow like meself
Should he ever come
And sit with a wag, chin wagging
Beside a diesel drum.

Kevin Meehan

15

Concrete Casualty

Slumped asleep in a darkened doorway
Missing children huddle up and shiver
The city is all they can call their home
Its streets are where their youth begins to whither
Slipping down poverty's spiral
Past the point of no return
Just one move social casualty
Of a Government with no concern
News of the world's suffering
Used to warm their soles.
A stray dog in tow for sympathy
Both just waiting for their bell to toll
Endless time spent searching meals
Begging for every crumb
Long nights with pangs of hunger
Leaving every sense so numb
And with corruption on every corner
Vultures loom over easy pray
Innocence exposed to danger
Young lives drugged make an easy lay
Two fingers stuck up in the air
At all those people who never stop
But always stare
At children with only cold concrete to rest their head
In this
Their cruel Conservative bed.

David Goldblatt

16

Sweet Sixteen

Sweet sixteen and never been kissed,
But I've been on the streets for a year.
Don't stand back in horror,
It's what we all do around here.

No, don't pretend you're bothered,
Or act like you really care,
If I came anywhere near your house,
I wouldn't be welcome there.

You're worried about my safety,
Out here, on the streets, alone?
Can't you believe what I suffered
In the 'sanctity' of my home?

No, sweet sixteen and never been kissed
And never been given a choice.
Can't sign on. Can't find a home.
And never been given a voice.

Sweet sixteen and wouldn't be missed.
Nothing to give and nothing to leave.
Will sweet sixteen make seventeen?
If not, would anyone grieve?

C D Stone

Homeless Women and the Young

There's a woman pushing a Safeway trolley.
She's certainly not a fashion model dolly!
Her possessions blankets and little else there!
Had she a home, a family and any who care!
Of all the people of the street life
Many are women. Were they ever a wife?
Men are often the victims of mugger and murderer true,
Yet women are often abused by men of equal poverty cue!
Sometimes their greatest enemy is the male down and out,
For he will be a 'pimp' and for customers tout!
Oh she's *nothing* give us a couple of quid mate,
She will oblige she's worth more, but she's great!
She is half drugged and maybe half drunk too!
She knows little of what is happening *true*.
For she is a pawn in the chess game of life,
She will be used, abused whether single or wife!
Life is not easy whether rich or poor,
There are always troubles at everyone's door,
But of all who live on the earth any day,
The women on the streets receive 'no fair play'.
The children who appear on streets too,
Are so often quickly abused into vice cue,
And many responsible are of the better class!
One would not expect such 'acts' by them to pass!
If only more people gave some thought!
Instead of sneers and self righteousness bought!
If all thought and tried to improve a little part,
If would create much help and give so many a hoping heart!

Tarbert

18

Homeless

Trapped in the cold dark well of despair
They sit. Hunched up. Knees bent. Eyes blind.
Waiting for someone to help them, to care
Not daring to hope that one will be kind.

Surviving, existing is all that they know,
And sit. Hunched up. Knees bent. Eyes blind.
Hearing the people who walk to and fro
Jingle the change that they can't seem to find.

A small piece of cardboard propped up at their feet,
They sit. Hunched up. Knees bent. Eyes blind.
Pleading for life to us here in the street
They remain without hope, and not daring to mind.

Why do we let our compatriots die?
Who sit. Hunched up. Knees bent. Eyes blind.
While we, safe and sound in the warm and dry,
Sit down and think of the things we can buy.
But they seem so honest, and we seem to lie
As we listen impassive to their lonely cry.
We know deep inside that we're both of a kind
But they sit alone and can see - we are blind.

S A H Robinson

19

Side Street

Now, the other side of the street
it's just the same really -
allowing for the sun catching it
different times. Good old sun.
Wind rain snow
don't particularise.
Straight up and down.

Drains smell the same, too.
Roughly. Bins distributed
pretty well on the famous
equi-distant principle -
breakfast a fair-play
number of steps.
Cordon Bleu's a bit irregular.

And, as I said,
both sides of the street
they're much the same.
Only, more people walk
on the other side.

Eric Morgan

In This House

In this house which is not my home
they have set up a new system called us and you, ours and yours
I think they're trying to tell me something rather important!

In this house they want to let me know that I don't belong
at least not if I stay as I am
they want me to become the person that lived here before
the one who understood that a friendly touch or a hug
only takes place between lovers and close friends
no matter what I'm used to

In this house there are lots of double standards
their possessions are decorative but mine are unsightly
(something which they never fail to remind me about)
support and unload means *listen* to us
but please don't tell us *your* troubles

In this house they want to integrate all things wrong (*me*)
into all things right (*them*)
it seems that I should understand all the unspoken limits
about friendship, attitudes, issues for discussion
and sharing - or Not as the case may be
am I suddenly telepathic?
anyhow I'm sure I don't want to be 'integrated'
if that's what it means

In this house which has never been my home
I am amazed at their blindness
they wonder why I don't seem to have settled in very well
why I enjoy only my own room so much
why I seem more relaxed around the company of my old friends
why I spend so many nights away

It's not that I don't have a *house* to go to
It's just that *this* house is definitely not a home

Andry Anastasiou

Sanctuary in the Underground

Sitting around human waste
Nursing a battered life displaced
Relevant to the brown blind mice
That run, head butting leather uppers.

Desperation of a deathly calm festers irritatingly
Upon a once sound, now eroding mind
As I seek a roof from the night fright
Where the surreal of mind linger
Around the bleakness of England's fallen.
Well to do, whatever they do, they won't do unto me.

This black tube line used to matter to me
But yesterday's gone on forever's holiday
Where distant memories bathe sublime
Not coloured, and vivid, but grey.

Like always they stared on the shell of my tramp
As I sat in the rays of a reassuring sun
Where their steps quickened across my shadow
And I was dreaming of robbery,
Escaping, to some distant land
Where life is easy, not trying.

But I haven't yet seen that brilliant light
At the end of my degrading plight
So I scavenge with the brown blind mice
That run head butting leather uppers.

Then with a flick of a positive thumb
A nicotine stick burns angrily,
In the place where I seek sanctuary
In the underground,
Until the time that I am moved
Back in the arms of the night fright
To the dark streets of England's fallen.

David Conway

A Lonely Existence

In this, my home
 - this park, this street corner
where my rooms have no walls
and my roof is the constantly changing sky.

I sit, looking through my windows
 - for these are the windows of the world.
I see the rush of briefcases trying to meet office deadlines,
I hear the rustle of taffeta skirts returning home from parties,
I smell the alcohol which accompanies the jeering insults of
                                                drunken gang warfare.

And I curl up - trying to turn my back on the cold
but nothing can warm the iciness which loneliness brings
I watch the thousands of people milling round my home
 - thousands of uninvited guests failing to acknowledge me,
                                                their host.

Maybe I do not exist, should not exist
 - all these blank faces staring me into invisibility -
                                        into insignificance.

Just what is so different about me?
What is it that sets me apart from them?
They could at least show me a little respect
 - after all, it is my home they are walking through.

Tania Venison

24

Concrete Person

At noon in the blazing hot sun embroiled,
slumped old and ill,
'faux' stone indifferent to all things,
fights life in the moving jungle of people and machines.

Radical flaws show from rusting cores;
minute tremblers vibrate the solid mass,
imperceptible to the fleeing hordes;
avoiding contact and presence with the degrading unstable crass.

Putrid, filthy, stinking clothing;
lichen and mosses cling to the bulwark,
lodged by the steps.
Fetid human debris and faeces lie scattered about,
abandoned without precepts.

Seasons wet and dry the fabric and body;
stiffening this bastion of irreverent isolation;
until night time and streetlights cause surreptitious yawns,
and the Concrete Person awakes to another night of anonymous
desolation.

Ben Dunk

Homeless

The empty doorway frames you like a picture; you huddle in its
corners.

The still life which is you looks out at the moving world.
Sometimes the world stops to stare, but usually it scurries by.
The wind blows round tormenting and relentless,
Whisking cans and wrappings down your street.
This is *your* street; your pitch closely guarded from intruders.
Owning nothing, you claim this doorway with your presence.
Grime and peeling paint aren't your choice of decor, nor tatters your
preferred clothes; but they're all you have.
So you rejoice in a dull, miserable gladness, a box would be worse.
A few people have less, but they are not few enough.
On Fridays you have cake and sandwiches; your eyes brighten as
you peer into the bag.
'Oh no, not corned beef again,' you say, the joking spirit flitting to the
surface.
Life is free, and fed and clothed . . . sometimes.
You knew a girl who heard voices, they followed her to your street.
She pleaded in your doorway and you offered a share.
Until her voices tried to get in too; there wasn't room for all of you.
Tormenting worse than the biting wind, sneering, they drove her to
the edge of her courage, but no-one could help.
She took herself away one day, but the voices went too,
And chased her, mocking, over the bridge.

You watch the rain drip down your glass; the picture blurs and you
recede from view.
Tomorrow you will still be there, but will we remember you?

Claire Beckmann

26

Everybody's Got Somewhere to Hide Except me and my Teddy

Bye-bye to
a dystopian haven.

Caged out of the silent steps
and a plastic Elysian field
and a humming concrete bridge
of snores, the chorus' kennel,
a sepulchral Collective.

Tabernacled,
a diluted cup
spills perverted
onto the street.

Bye-bye to
a garbaged wishbone.

Lullabyed by halfpenny chimes
and flash windowfuls of techno
and finger-tapping tunes
of cashpoints, the only music,
a song of ignorance.

Bedded,
love-me-nots propagate
wilts and withers,
slurred into alcoves.

Night-night to
a teddy-bear memory.

Surrendered,
another day,
spills perverted
into tomorrow.

Ciarán Crilly

Down Town

Fooling sense, a duplicitous dusk
Finds me down in Acton Town
Dirty cotton clouds swab over
To muffle crying memories.
Sleep half waking, waking sleep
 - my mother would she hold me now
Or as one adult to another speak.

Too many houses pass me by
Like somewhere else I can hardly see
Painted doorjambs, shutters, blinds
Mixed up with a remembered dream.
Here half gone, going gone
Leaving a trail of withered roots
A dusty footprint
Rotting shoots.

Joanna Gilbrook

Untitled

Runaway, runaway
Runaway from home
Escape from the prison
That once was your dream.
Run to where
Where can you go
Why run to a prison
That is greater than home.

Down on the streets
You'll have plenty of time
To reflect . . . to remember
The time that's passed by.
Don't turn to drink
You'll only sink deeper
The street is a prison
And drink the chains.

Look up - don't you see,
Listen - don't you hear.
There is freedom waiting for you.
Break down the barrier.
Climb over the wall
Forgive and forget
Then follow your call.

Runaway - runaway
Don't run from home.
Break out of the prison
That has enslaved your soul.

D J Andrews

No Face

I try to imagine
Those people without homes
And how they must feel:
Cold,
Hungry,
Alone,
And tired . . .
Tired of the faces looking the other way . . .
Tired of the insults and jeers . . .
Tired of the pitying stares . . .
Tired of being a person without a face
Instead of just a person without a home.

I try to ignore
The feeling that builds up within me
But it refuses to go away:
The Guilt
The Shame
The Horror
Of the knowledge that I am one of those faces who looks away,
One of those who laughs and mocks,
On of those with patronising looks of pity,
And then I realise . . .
It is I who has no face.

Pauline Middleton

31

On a London Street

Cloaking the fragility of my soul
My hide
The torn cardboard box wherein I lie.
And dazed in torment look above
The disposed needles of the dispossessed.
In the gutter clutter of a London lost,
To all but greedful opulence.
They have,
We have not.
Malcontents or lost?
We care not which.
We have no lost or found office.
Our address?
Post restante for the DHSS.
For the rest?
We do not exist.
Seeing they pass us
We, the unseen, cry:
'Save the environment
But spare the cardboard box!
Build banks;
To house the fraudsters fraud?
Allow:
All mental hospitals to close.'
Let the inmates come -
From mad houses - to,
The City of the Mad.
Within this fine brutality
Snare mutes.

Richard Cheevers

Plight

Stumbled out into moving traffic
In a haze of alcoholic delusion
If the cap fits wear it
If an odd plimsoll does not
Still wear it
They make an arc
Around a still body
Laying on the path
One leg missing at the knee
Still they pass
Chirping on about a new dilemma
I ask if I can help
They recoil at the oozing stump
I can't really help this time
Three nines later
And I move away
Poor old bugger in the Saville Row cast offs.

Ian Hicks

Change Please

This morning,
I sat under the bridge,
To keep out of the rain.
The public's conscience
Amounted to:
Five pfennigs
One French Franc
An old Ten p
A stale cigarette
Twenty p
A dozen glares
And unlimited abuse.

You say I'm scared of work,
But how many hours
Would you do for that?

J A Lelliott

In a City

The wind rumbles the belly
Of the old house.
Condensation drips black
Into the woodwork.
Across the papered walls
Tulips shed their petals,
Uncurtained grime
Veils the windows.
Knife-edged time
Has scraped the palette dry,
Flaked the paint
From empty room to empty room.
Alone the carpets unravel
Their mysteries of fruit and flower.

Irena Uderska

The Pigeon

You live off the waste and decay of mankind
Ugly little grey thing that begs so earnestly.
No home, no warmth, diseased and despised
You patrol your station, strut so proudly
An old graceful gentleman.
That discarded ham sandwich, an ancient crisp
May be your first meal in weeks, may be your last.
No concept of time, you only watch the evercoming trains,
Show off your skills, walking on roofs, braving the track.
It gets cold, so cold.
Then you entertain,
Fouling on the innocent commuter
You're such a filthy creature, yet
It would be strange not to see you.

Sarah Kent

36

Waterloo Bridge

Waterloo Bridge
Lincoln Inn Fields,
Some of the places that some people know.
Some of the places that homeless people can no longer go.

They gather in groups but still stand alone,
No food in their stomach, no bed and no home.
Buildings stand empty and going to waste,
But yet they still build?

How much money would it cost,
Compared to the lives that are lost?
The people who are helping and giving their all,
Make the people with power, look small.

There are people who talk.
And people who do.
And action will always speak
Louder than words . . .
(C C)

Lester Dunstan

Conspiracy

They are burning the guy years later.
Hatred, the acrid hiss of blistered memories,
Dries into the whisper of a breathless sky.
The air snaps over the brittle twigs.
Waiting.

Like a man who has lived in the streets,
He huddles with his head half turned,
Spreads coarse fingers over crackling paper,
Listens for rain.
The faint, sharp crack of a cigarette lighter
Teases him until his eyes are viscous
Paraffin.
The flames incite the dry branches
Set in their gnarled ways.
The wind circles the pyre,
Bribed by their spitting voices,
Until flickering crowds of fire
Clamber to sear the stained, creased skin.

Later, years later,
He burns again,
Watches the sparks melt,
The unlit firework smoulder,
The anniversary of failure,
Buried in parchment leaves
Before his gleam fades
In the spluttering embers,
In narrow-eyed anger.

Deborah Binstock

Steve 004

I bought his magazine
And had his story thrown in.
The gist of it being,
He'd hit London full of hope
But wound up homeless -
Robbed on the Southend train.
He blamed himself for this,
Rueful yet cheerful.
His chatter, patter and charm were still intact,
But he'd known loneliness alright,
It was in his poem -
Oh! Did I say poem?
I've let it out of the bag too soon for a punchline.
But then so did he,
Rummaging in his rucksack
For the right crumpled page,
And he stood as I read,
A picture of pleasure and pure pride.

Mary Healy

A Stereo-Typical Image

Brown woollen hat, ragged, threadbare,
forms no contrast with the rest of his shabby attire.
From day to day, he sustains a look that any
middle-class grunge fan would be proud of.
In the precinct, he has just one friend,
a mangy, smog-coloured poodle.
It's sad, dark eyes are the only ones he really
ever sees. His own sullen pair remain transfixed -
rarely moving from the filthy down trodden pavement.
Oppressed is his life.

The torn back of an ancient cornflake packet
lies at his feet, flapping, being battered by
the chilling, powerful wind (if only it had the power to change
                                          his plight).

His request is propped up with an old pebble
from Brighton beach - a single reminder of
a different, happier life.
The card bears the black markered inscription:
'Any spare change, please?'

His one simple question,
but what is your answer?

Chloë Pinchin (16)

40

The Homeless Omelette

Early in the morning (it was still dark)
I sneaked into the back of a McDonald's
And stole an egg (one of hundreds).

I went to a nearby dustbin
And, with a flourish,
Cracked the egg on the edge
And emptied it onto the rubbish.

Maybe I thought I was doing a Floyd special
For the homeless:
'If you're on the street and need to eat,
An omelette is a simple treat.
Take two eggs, empty into a dustbin and stir.

'Of course you could not eat the result,
But maybe you will find *something* in there
Which will help you.'

Daniel S Brichto

The Camera Never Lies

There I am, in the corner of the frame,
The unintentional star of a holiday video.
I'll bet when you booked your City break
You didn't expect to take my brown bulk home
Captured for prosperity on camcorder.
Like a news report on Sudan followed by a juggling cat
The impression gets distorted.
You're upset? I'll bet you are, I spoil the shot,
But videoing in London, it's hard to avoid me and my like.
We are here in numbers, but not by choice.
Hey, why should I complain?
My face on your TV screen over and over again.
This is the first time I've been in a living room for six years.
I'm nineteen years old.

Steve Dyche

Concrete City

The gold rush and poor amble
the same council slabs,
that rain brings umbrellas
from Waterloo and traps

But money and no time,
don't drop coins in caps

So time and no money
watch rain

drop down concrete gaps

Ruth Johannsen

The Travelling Man

The travelling man
Homeless
Moves through the dust
Kicked up by the heels
Of desperation
Lost
Trying to find clean air
High on the hill
Unseen
Through the haze of anger
Frustration
Locked in a state of depression
Understood by Him?
The travelling men
Joined
By their own mobile
Crucifix.

Jim Parkinson

Homeless

Giving homeless names of places to wander streets
Nowhere to go, no stairs to climb or sheets to lay a frown upon
Line after line of old oil drums spitting smoke 'til the fires done
Line after line of cardboard boxes under bridges where railways run.

Puddles splash, old men with blackened teeth.
Fitfully sleeping a face with twitches of the human race.
Cardboard streets this night, this night he sits and looks at rain
As it slips beyond a tearful face.
Tears swell in eyes that tell an untold story.
Rays of the past the unconcerned glory life giving into the
Truth.

Leaving his cardboard slum walking wet streets, will the nightfall
come?

Michael Boyle

The Best of British Farce

Sporting prose-tinted glasses
You stroll down The Strand;
Clutching passes for farces
You pass by my hand.

Open Hand
Closed Eyes
Closed Hearts

Does the frost on your glasses
Mask my frost-bitten hand?
Or like one of these farces
Are you soulless and bland?

Noises Off
Noses Up
Switch Off

'Oh, the poor underclasses . . . '
You don't understand!
While you sit on your arses
It is *dying*, this land;

My Land
Your Land
Soon No-Man's

While you *Run For Your Wife*
I must beg for my *life*.

James Mortleman

Home

I found a home, it's called a box.
It's not very big, but it has a door,
A sleeping bag and a candle. A hotel
For one.
I have my servants. They clean the street.
My job is people, their money is a special
Treat.
A portion of chips, a cup of tea. A palatable
Meal. It's pretty neat.
No electric bills for me; street light is
Enough you see.
When it rains or snows, I pick up my box
And move address. I find a bridge. It's
Quite picturesque.
What a life: the great outdoors, Mother Nature
And her chores.
She helps me when I'm cold. Gives me Summer and
Velvet blanket grass.
One day when I'm richer, I shall have a bigger box,
And a sleeping bag made for two.

Nicholas Aristotelous

Drowning on Dry Land

My feet are on firm ground,
But I'm sinking fast.
There's no way out
Of this situation that I'm in.
It's all a mess.
There's no light at the end of the tunnel
And I'm sinking fast.
Nothing to hold on to
No one to pull me back,
It's a no end situation
And I'm in it up to my neck
They all ask me what's wrong
And I tell them,
Me, I'm drowning on dry land.

Nichola Kinnersley

Begging

Making my way back
Through London, I saw . . .
Young girl, blonde hair
Same age as me
Sitting, hunched over
Alone on the dirty pavement
Asking passers-by for change
Money to spare.

She looked at me
And asked the question
To look back
I did not dare

Instead, heavy bag in hand
I shifted my attention elsewhere
Walked on by
As though I didn't care
When underneath I did wonder

- What was she really doing there?

Fiona Tait

The Ignorance of the Ignorant

He never asked to be homeless,
He never asked to be poor,
He never asked to spend his nights,
In front of a shop door.

And they call him a dosser,
They call him a slob,
They shout, 'Get off the pavement.
Get yourself a job.'

He tries to close his ears,
But it cuts to the core
When the ignorance of the ignorant
Is so hard to ignore.

He walks in the sunshine,
Yet stares at the ground,
Ashamed he lets their proud
Superiority get him down.

The society who made him
Quickly pass by near,
Looking straight through him,
Pretending they don't hear.

It's not the change that bothers him
(Though he needs it more they)
It's the knowledge he'll be doing this
Every single day.

Until one day we realise
It can go on no more,
Then the ignorance of the ignorant
Will be easy to ignore.

Natasha Morris

A Vagrant

'Y' get used to it.
Well, y' have to . . . to survive.
The life aint that bad
Ther aint no problems, no worries.
'Cept gettin' yer next fag 'er sumthin'.
There's always the soup kitchen.

'Aye, the summer's the best,
No worries, no problems, life just drifts along.
People're friendlier, more generous too.
They give ther money with a smile, sometimes.
The sun's out, the birds 'r' in the park
That's nice - feelin' the warmth, watchin' people go by
Not too hard to sleep at night, downrite pleasant actchaly'.

'Spose winter's the worst,
That's when most of 'em buy it.
The cold gets locked in yer bones and don't leave
And the wind whistles straight through - i'taint nice.
But you'could stand it were it no fer the wet.
That's what gets 'em.
Someuns just give it up
Starin' up t'the sky like ther seein' God Almighty're somethin'
It's not nice'.
It's a damn shame.

Paul McAvoy

Hope (the Futility of Hope)

A pink and purple sky floating over a shabby brown street
A shrouded moon my heart still beats
I hide within for fear of falling
To the place from which dead souls are calling
Me to join them in despair
T'would be easy to be ensnared
Remind myself to take due care
For the places from which they beckon
Are not the places for me I reckon

Lives are wasted often
Is it then for me to soften
The fall that waits for thoughtless mortals
Or should I pass through other portals

As I watch with deepened sorrow
I can only hope and dream and borrow
Visions of another land
Where people roam hand in hand
Where lies are not a means of living
Where all with love they do the giving
Is it really all a dream
Or is it sadly as it seems

Hope forgotten and despised
No one caring no one tries
Living lives of mediocrity
Does no one realise the hypocrisy
Of modern life in all it's glory
Will you listen now to my story

Stuart Arden

Homeless

A man sat in a doorway, head bowed,
Shoulders hunched defensively,
Wrapped in a shroud of silence,
While all around him traffic hooted,
Wheels turned, engines roared
And life went on relentlessly.
Feet tapped or plodded by,
And from time to time,
Loose change spilled guiltily
From the pocket or purse
Of some well-meaning passer-by.
Too tired to lift his eyes,
Too tired to look for justice,
The man sat alone and stared
At the endless colourful parade
Of shoes and socks filing past
Mingling with jumbled voices
In the fume-filled city air.

Beryl Stockman

Expression

That man standing on the corner
Like an angel
Jammed between the crowd
And the apathy of the world

A Aranda

Tramp

What is it I see here
This vague and vapid stare?

An escapee from the nose
  Would captivate -
Capture attention around here!

Mr Meths, in all his untidiness;
  Finger shaped pockets,
Woe wrinkles around his eyes

Commands no light of day
No respite from his monotony,
Just wants to fade away.

But, he hurts too
Feels that stinging teardrop,
Too far gone to stop.

What is it I see here
A tramps flint-eyed glare?

Paul Lumsden

Old Delhi Awakens

City dawns with clashing colour.
Saris orange, tika powder,
Chandni Chowk breathes like a flower.

Bridge buttress and roadside spaces
Heave with limbs, of homes no traces,
Delhi born and far-flung places.

Plainsman gaunt from Uttar Pradesh,
Lithe Punjabi with just a dash
Of optimism and panache.

Diminutive Bengali grins,
He left his family to win
Rupees, road labour long and grim.

He may return after success,
Or stay for ever with excess,
The next day's work his only stress.

Mother squatting with two young girls,
No husband, these unwanted pearls,
If just one son, he'd share their dahl.

Their home could be a shanty town,
But cruelly they've been disowned,
So beg they must and dream of home.

We grasp their hands, proffer rupees,
Brown eyes light up with anxious plea
To pray for them on bended knee.

The pavement's hard, the winter cold
With grime encroaches, acting bold
It cuts their marrow, death takes hold.

One hates the world at times like this,
What miracle can bear their cross
And shape their life to one of bliss?

David Carter

57

Des Res

They're queuing up for cardboard boxes under Waterloo:
there's a waiting list.
It's highest offers only in sealed envelopes for each
sought-after pitch.

They make a fortune out of begging,
they buy special clothes with holes in
go to workshops to learn shivering, humility
and how to look appealing to the punters.
They rake it in.

So please don't give them money, they've got plenty
and it only does more harm than good -
they'd spend it all on drink
and drugs or gamble it away
on fruit machines.

And it's no good trying to clean them up
or put them in a proper place,
they'd just come back like homing pigeons
straight away as quick as wink before you could say
homelessness.

They're jostling for first go in the dustbins in the Strand:
there's a feast in there.
They're dining lavishly out of litter bins, no charge
for the soup round.

There is no excuse for starving nowadays,
it's just the way they choose to live
they don't pay taxes and they all get
loads of hand-outs from the government
they don't like work.

Oh it's comfy on the pavement in the drizzle in the winter
when you're swaddled in a bin bag in your corrugated home:
the queues are growing.

Susan Utting

Voices

Can you . . .
I just wond . . .
Could you sp . . .
I'm only asking . . .
A little-
Please I . . .
Could you . . .
Just . . .
Help me to . . .
Can you . . .
For food . . .
Could you . . .
I'm only asking . . .
Could you
Just
Help me to
Find a
Voice
That you
Will
Listen to?

David Hallen

A Bed of Daffodils

In a bed of daffodils he lay,
Hungry, wet, cold, alone.
There from dawn to dusk each day,
He had no friends or home.

His face was old, his hair was grey,
all withered, tired and worn.
A tough life he had, no place to stay,
Unhappy and forlorn.

I often think about this man,
so dismal, poor and sad.
I wonder how his life began,
And will it end so bad?

Now under a bed of daffodils,
Peaceful and sleeping sound.
He lies there quiet, happy and still,
deep beneath the ground.

Julia Black

Too Much Money

Oh! How I wish I had,
too much money!
How I'd be glad!
Now I only have one small car,
(and one for the wife!)
Oh! What a horrible life!
Fashion changes all the time,
trying to keep up is such a bind!
Always, there's work to be done
and bills to paid,
there's no time for fun, I'm afraid,
except, of-course, for pub,
Badminton and restaurants, for grub.
I spend restless nights,
my bed is too hard,
pillow's too small,
I'm surprised I sleep at all!
My wife's put on three more stone,
this year alone!
We eat more than we should,.
we'd cut down, if we could.
So when I see those homeless types,
whinging their miserable gripes,
I'd like to tell them how poor I am!
When they beg through lack of food,
I'd like to tell them,
without being too rude:
'I have no money to spare,
I need it more than you, so there!'
If you need help, don't ask me,
I'm just your average business man,
you see!

(and if you don't like what's just gone,
then go out and prove me wrong!)

Richard A Poynton

Untitled

To you, the sirens are on the screen.
But, they are in the street outside your window,
Piercing your cocoon of pretence.

No one screams in your house.
Your heart lives on the mantelpiece;
An empty frame.

Can the sounds of the outside touch you?
Ignorant silence is a torturous weapon;
What happened to the scream in you?

Jo Bryan

Destitute

No dignity left, no pride,
the sleeping bag a shroud,
into which he escapes,
the harsh reality,
of the cold December day,
and his dreary, bleak future.

The dull eyes stare blankly,
yet drink in the contempt,
complete strangers pass by,
unconcerned and uncaring,
on route to warm homes,
families and food on the table.

Every day the same,
a struggle for survival,
no money, no home,
the drowning victim,
he lies forgotten,
in the debris of Society's wasteland.

Lisa Owen

A Song for all Seasons and St Vitus' Dance

It's too hot in the sun, in the shade its too cold
The pavements are glittering, broken glass, fools gold
How was I to know a gut fooling would turn into gutter dreams
The stuffings been knocked out of me I've been torn apart at the
seams

The seasons used to come and go now they've turned into one
Christmas carols drift in the air along with summers song
I'm running out of time of rhyme and reason
Singing the same old song for the same old season

Hands in my pockets a jacks and some change
My collars pulled up to fend off the rain
I feel better outside in the chill morning air
Anything's better than another half hour in there
Really thought I'd lost it clutched onto the table
Well past the state of disorderly, more like disabled
A wilting wallflower in a strange place looking for romance
Red eye and legless, reduced to St Vitus' Dance

As I've walked past Kings Cross, St Pancras and Euston
I've thought of going back but to go back would be useless
Now they've taken the room, cassette player and telly away
I'm walking round with the ghost of a Lord Mayors cat on cup final
day
All we've found here is my Nadir, all that's for left me to do
Is send it away for the rest of the day with tenants Kessie or Brew
It's then I'll sing that song for all seasons and perchance
You'll pass by and see me lost in St Vitus' Dance

Stevie Hooper

The Place

Still.
Silent.
Ghostly ministry that moves the leaf
And sieves my hair.
Calm.
Collected.
Flapping images that hover close by.
Black, grey, green, red this banquet for my eye.
Searching, scavenging creatures
In need of wholesome stuff
Beat the olive twig against the tree,
Battering, slapping leaves in
Mind - bent frenzie
Ingenious ones ascending heights
To clasp the fruit - born branch
To taste the stuff there of.
Clinging, clasped footed
To avoid the inevitable descent
Back, so far back
To the scavenger's pit.
Such silent folly.
A public place theatre
Played before my lens.
Cruel but calm.
Searching in silence.
The scavengers stay
Then take wings and
Fly away.

Nik Williams

Homelessness

They put us onto the street,
they stacked our possessions
round our feet, as we sat
the baby on my lap, the
children's eyes so frightened,
and our hopelessness drifting
round us in waves of mist.
Then came the echoes of despair
in the sharp shrill air.
The children were quiet, their
eyes sad and solemn, carrying
their Teddy bears and toys,
forlorn in their plight, small
and frightened. The people
stared at our souls laid
bare, and at our humiliation
and our sorrow, and our
unknown tomorrow.

Diana Radcliffe

Untitled

My body went hard against honey-moon cities,
Whipping us into alien corners filled with
Tanks of angel-fish. Awakening, at night,
Outside, I made a deal; my temple
sucked by the white breast - with its many
antennae. Or rather I was in a palace
of primroses that choke on their tongues,
And was in fact reading a book of jokes.
Later, I discovered a tattoo on my shoulder of
magnolia, which informed me that I had not
taken enough care; or as you may say - one
head can drink much more sugar than two
In hunting expeditions through cowardly heaven.
Central celebrations were struck up! - Because
I had needed no help in losing something as
large as heaven - I did not refuse to join them.
Using all my senses outside the highest tower,
I noticed that, by night, the human child folds
Its wings back, against its body, and falls freely
into the kiss of nightmares. Perhaps, indeed,
If I may be so bold as to stutter the
mosaic of words: a girl might get her hair
coiled round in plants. Whilst in March I
allowed bowlfuls of nothing to hurtle,
unceremoniously, into my orphan's mouth.
Innocently as little red riding hood I guffawed
in the tear-stained faces of nymphs clustered
around the ashes of a party - but all the
time my fist was metaphorically clenched.

John Ash

Homeless (on My Bench)

Sat on my bench, there's nowhere to sleep
Just sat here feeling, dirty and cheap
No money, no food, and nothing to drink
I can smell the world, the stench, the stink
I feel just like, a missing link

There's just nowhere, to call my home
I feel like a nomad, forever to roam
Lots of strange faces, looking at me
Walking the streets, got no dignity
Please help me God, to find my liberty

No hope, just gloom and bloody despair
No bed, just living in the open air
Long cold nights, with no one to cuddle
My mind and life in such a muddle
As on my bench I sit and huddle

No one to love, there's just no hope
I might as well, go and find some rope
Find a train, that'll kill the pain
There's no one here, there's no one there
What a life, no kit to fix, or even repair

No soap, no rope, no hope, and me, I just can't cope
Trying to cross this bloody moat

Peter David Brown

Insanity

You know you cannot hide away from us
We are your mind and insecurities
Hear the harbingers of delirium
The darkness will consume your spirit
Come with us into Pandemonium
We will deliver you from misery
Succumb to us and free your inner soul
Adhere to the voices that beckon you
To leave the bedlam of society
Annex with us into another grace
And take the path towards insanity.

Angela Chung

At the Station Coffee Shop

Among the ebbing and flowing of travellers
A lady sat, still, in the coffee shop.
Trains arrived,
departed,
without her.
I came to rest at a nearby table.
Her smile shone across at me
and my flowers,
Flowers for my mother.
We spoke then
of mothers, sisters, childhood,
home.
Home is where the heart is after all.
As my train arrived and I rose to leave
I wanted her to have my flowers.
But she would not take them.
'Give them to your mother,'
she said,
'Take them home.'

Tracy Radley

Homelessness

Gazing with glazed unseeing eyes
Hunched low and cold against the wall
Grey splinters of November rain penetrate to my soul
Washing away the last remnants of my dignity
Dirty, wet, bedraggled
Unloved
Unwanted
Seen only by a few
Ignored by thousands
Somebody else's problem
Life wasn't always like this
I used to hold my head up high
Look my fellow man in the eye
What does he care for me now
Life - *what life?*

D J Beer

Untitled

Damp dark coldness here
A winter morning soupline
Cardboard city stirs

H Jefferis

Damn you People

Damn you people,
I say as they go by.
Can't you see us
Hello, we are here.

Look we're flesh and blood,
Just like you,
Except homeless and cold,
Do you have a heart,
Yes, you, just look in the mirror and you shall know who.

See that lady with her child
Saying, 'Please give me some money, my child is hungry,'
That man over there with no clothes is dying.
Yes, just as I thought your heart is still cold.

Wait until you come by next time,
There won't be none of them here,
Just a dead corpse,
Don't you understand there is no next time for us!

Looking in dustbins for food,
Young girls turning to prostitutes,
Others on drugs and alcohol,
This trouble to stay alive.

All we ask is a few measly pennies,
From each one of you,
It can buy us food and save our lives,
But without you we have no one.

Are you still cold hearted,
Or do you feel for these people,
Whatever you feel,
I try and help the homeless and please do the same!

Shelpa Ladva

Humanity

Seal so innocent and still
Some mother's baby which she cannot hide
The enemy closes in without humanity
One smash on his scull and he is killed.

Gentle giants ride the sea
The whaling ships draws in so close
Twang the harpoon flies through the air
Piercing their bodies blood runs free

Battery hens in rows pecking for food.
Heads pushed through rough troughs
Never seeing the light of day
Closing in on them what is their mood

Dogs in braces with soft small cry
How can they defend themselves
Stuffing smoke down the throat into lungs
Until it's time to say goodbye.

Why are we so cruel and ruthless.
Tormenting these creatures without love
Not asking to be brought into this world
It just proves that this world is in an attrocious mess.

Margaret Rose

Mr Nobody

He is laying in a doorway
on the street,
attempting to keep warm
with old newspapers
wrapped around his feet.

Condemned to another
fitful night,
as the dampness
begins to seep,
through his ragged clothes.

He tries to remember how
he ever came to be like this,
but his alcohol soaked brain
scatters his memories,
like the passers by
splashing through
the puddles in the rain.

They choose to ignore
the figure huddled
in the shop door,
not wishing to think
it could ever happen to them,
blotting out the reality
not daring to even offer
the price of a cup of tea.

All through the night
he lays there,
cramped and withdrawn
not even stirring,
at the first sign of dawn.

A milkman on his rounds
notices that something
is not quite right,
and then as he races
to find a telephone,
he is struck by the sadness
of someone dying so alone.

Paul Kelly